There's a little ambiguity over there among the bluebells

1968
Something Else Press, Inc.
New York / Toronto / Frankfurt-am-Main

There's a little ambiguity over there among the bluebells
and other theater poems
by Ruth Krauss
graphics by Marilyn Harris

This is a Krauss sampler disorganized to turn you on to the possibilities of selection and juxtaposition and creating your own show. The theater pieces have been set to music, published and widely performed at Judson Poets Theater, Café Cino, Café la Mama, Actors Studio, etc. – *the editor*

Weather

Cloudy with occasional immaculate conception today.

Drunk Boat

act one everyone is born
act two South Pole
act three West 86th Street
act four everyone contracts
act five everyone recovers
act six everyone dies

Act seven
because seven is a magic number
the torch carriers are waiting on the side

TORCH SONG

Life, the girls are wearing their skirts higher
    and higher
    for you
Life, at the South Pole the icebergs
    are dancing for you
For you the film-makers are making films
And me I am writing a poem
    for you
    look! no hands—
I be carry for you torch great torch set on fire whole world
    waterfalls green lightnings maelstrom
    unlatched land and the tree that will become a violin
    or perhaps a fence
Life, I am eyes full of accolades for you
    my ocean
    my moon
    my horse

a great meadow appears
the clown riding a broomstick-with-wings comes
galloping over it
"Pardon me, Sir" he says to the broomstick
"I thought you was a horse"

the broomstick takes off from under
the clown and flies away

CLUNK MAN
Clunk!

NARRATOR: in a poem you make your point with lemons-on-fire

LEMONS-ON-FIRE fly out overhead across the
horizons over into onto the stage from all
directions the people run out and bow lie down
and roll in the grass on the rooftops in the sand

ICEBERG: and it would be nice to have an iceberg going
in and out

Narcissus

NARCISSUS: How much do you love me how much

IMAGE: As much as tomato soup

NARCISSUS: Help!
            Send Help!

    Runners start running
    People jump out of windows
    Cabbages jump out of the ground
    There's a crucifixtion . . .

NARCISSUS: ?????

IMAGE: ?????

CABBAGES: ?????

?????: ?????

   ?

News

A crowd of twenty-three thousand coy mistresses is expected to turn out this morning for the forty-four day ruby-finding meet by the Indian Ganges' side. Eighth race on the card is scheduled for quaint honor to succumb to the tide at 4:35 P.M. and will be telecast. Thus while her willing soul transpires, she who wins shall take her due except she come up with the same bruised thigh that put her out of action last week.

Questions or maybe Answers

CHILD
Grandfather, do old people grow down
as young people grow up?

GRANDFATHER
Of course not, child.

(the grandfather begins to grow down his knees
are shortly framed in flowers his gold watch chain
his beard and now like Whitman full of butterflies

Trio

whom does the little one favor
whom does the little one favor

the little one favors the moon

whom does the little one favor
whom does the little one favor

the little one favors a young lettuce leaf

whom does the little one favor
whom does the little one favor

the little one favors the East River
and the Queensborough Bridge
and a beard full of butterflies
    a beard full of butterflies
that's whom the little one favors

Horse-Opera-With-Wings

Here comes the poet a-riding riding riding
Here comes the poet a-riding
on a HORSE-WITH-WINGS

POET: what a poet wants is—

THE HORSE takes off from under the POET and
        flies away

CLUNK MAN: Clunk

If Only

If only I was a nightingale singing
If only I was on my second don't-live-like-a-pig-week
If only the sun wasn't always rising behind the next hill
If only I was the flavor of tarragon
If only I was phosphorescence and a night phenomena
      at sea
If only Old Drainpipe Rensaleer as we used to call him
      hadn't hit bottom in Detroit the time he made
      a fancy dive and got absentminded and forgot
      to turn and all his shortribs got stove in he
      got sucked down the drainpipe because the grate
      wasn't on
If only I didn't have to get up and let our dog out now
If only the glorious day in April because it has no
      beginning or end that all Flatbush had awaited
      impatiently between creation and construction
      has come
If only I was James Joyce and had written Finnegans Wake
      only then I'd be gone
If only it was I had been cornerstone of the Parnassian
      edifice
If only I too had the force to batter a reader about
      like a shuttlecock and then strike him or her
      out with an indelible phrase to make him or her
      forever after a changed him or her
If only somebody would hug me right now
If only I was a sickle moon only then I'd never be full
If only I could explode like Symbolism
If only on the other hand I never explode like Symbolism

If only I was rain in the highest branches
If only I was a little stairs running straight up out
      of the sea
If only somebody would kiss me on the back of the neck
      right now
If only somebody would complain to *me*
        "Je n'ose pas me plaindre, ô maîtresse ingrate;
        Vous êtes sans oreille et je perdrais mon cris."
If only I hadn't read the Consumer's Report on the
      Chicken Industry
If only those degraded bastards hadn't monkeyed around
      with the Oreo Sandwich pattern
If only I didn't have to get up and let our dog in
      again now
If only Alicia had never answered the phone that day
If only Dudley didn't go around thinking she's the
      infant Jesus because she was born on Christmas and
      we should have a parade
If only I didn't think I was the infant Jesus otherwise
      what was I doing hanging upside down in a blue
      light in the barn all night
If only Gold's Delicatessen was on Chestnut River Road
If only New York City was in Connecticut
If only I had not said no to just lunch
If only I had said no to just lunch
If only we had not had to have our picnic sitting in the
      middle of the bridge
If only I too could be reassisted and rise up in the
      clocks that are moving saying 'Rainbow,
      rearrange yourself' and the precious stones
      crying out in envy 'Oh aha!' And in the forest
      lip daughters orange and kneeling in the clear
      deluge heavy with nakedness that makes her in
      the shade the flower

If only I was a plum
If only the seagulls would stop dropping clamshells
          on our roof
If only the girl and boy who all summer
          were walking the roads hand in hand
          and all autumn were walking the roads
          hand in hand and all winter are walking
          the roads hand in hand and all spring what on earth
          is going to happen to them hand in hand if only
          it stopped here and they could never
          know
If only I had never seen a shining river pouring
          out of the sky
If only the new rational interpretation for the Dodgers
          was not unfolding for a formal christening
If only I had never been a part of that almost completely
          human story where second base like the marrow of
          its bones mounted on air
If only Charlie Ebbets would go away
If only I didn't have so much electricity
If only I was a farm only I'd be sure to be
          a farm full of onions and pigs
          instead of a delightful acre of
          young green lettuces
If only I was a really sharp operator
If only I didn't forget the eggs every time I boiled them
If only I didn't forget the toast every time I boiled it
If only our dog wasn't such a pest and what was he doing
          anyway riding through the air all night in a white
          closed limousine
If only I had looked down that hole in Yucatan
If only I knew whether to wave at second hand Plymouths

If only somebody was following me down a street in Paris
       right now
If only a thousand poetry students dressed like sheiks
       would ride motorcycles down the street in front
       of our house right now
If only I was dawn
If only I was a drunken boat sailing between the lines
If only I was more mystically charged than blackest night
If only the little boy wearing glasses hadn't asked
       me if I was a witch
If only they didn't throw crackers around every morning
       and when it's not that it's dried apricots
If only I wasn't so interested in the Emperor's marriage
If only when you left them alone for ten minutes they
       didn't burn down the house
If only they would stop pursuing me to the four passions
       of the soul namely joy hope grief and fear
If only it was I who had invented suitable images
       of California
If only I was Socrates only then I'd be gone
If only he had never called me one of those who come
       into the world with a ray of moonlight in
       their brains
If only I was a little shell full of roaring
If only I lived in a little red caboose
If only men wouldn't commit bigamy for me
I only I had not seen the pushcart peddlar out selling
       me in a quarter edition translated by James Joyce
       last night
If only I had not played the violin until after
If only bigamy would go away
If only trigamy would go away

If only our dog would stop staring at me
If only they had never moved me farther out into the
       Western Ocean
If only my dream would not rise and fall by the moon
If only there were no chimneys in it
       'and a bird is flying by under a chimney in it?'
       'and a duck is sitting on itself in it'
       'and a sun is rising under the duck?'
       'and a sun is rising under the duck'
       'under the falling?'
       'rising under the falling'
       'the falling'
       'the falling'
       'and the moon again'
       'the moon again'
       'moon again'
       'moon'
If only I had never read that Space too is warped
If only my source too was in the mountain
If only I could forget that nifty number with a beautiful
       haircut everything working right doing her
       half-Veronicas out there with a mink stole and
       absolutely devastating the bull she had the
       sweat running out of the palms of my hands
If only she hadn't killed a hundred and fifty-eight bulls
If only I too could do half-Veronicas out there with
       a mink stole
If only Milwaukee hadn't been on its can during the
       Depression

If only he hadn't told me that a dog represented a
        father to me
If only France was in Connecticut
If only England was in Connecticut
If only Connecticut was in Turkey
If only Turkey was in Tierra del Fuego
If only I too was words on the page but much more
        a music that exists off the page
If only Connecticut was in France
If only I was in France
If only I was in Vallauris
If only Vallauris was in me
If only Picasso was in Connecticut
If only Connecticut was in Picasso
If only I was in Picasso
If only Picasso no! once a companion always a companion
If only I could bark louder
If only I had read the Consumer's report on green mascara
If only I wasn't tougher than a night in jail
If only once again the mountain was covered with peaches
If only once again for me green lace tangles
        were storming in the sea
If only once again the petticoats were flying down
        116th Street
If only I had known how convenient it was to be a baby
If only hallo Al! I fal from my shall
If only we hadn't taught Hero's father how to get peanuts
        out of keyholes

If only I hadn't had to climb the mountain last night
     with my head tucked underneath my arm
If only he hadn't been Catholic
If only once again I could comb my hair and it would
     stand up stiff in a crown of icicles instead
     of thorns
If only I knew what the woman in the night meant when
     the messenger from the wars raced up to her holding aloft
     the mass of pink ribbons with among them a black
     whip and she cried 'O look! My belt! He brings
     me fair girdle'
If only I was a really neat hustler
If only I could go skiing in the Virgin Islands
If only I am never a lion in front a goat in the middle
     and a serpent behind infesting mountains
If only he had not had a wife and six children
If only I could strike gold in me I guess I'd know it
If only I was a band full of bells
If only memory was like a chalk drawing
If only memory is never like a chalk drawing
If only we had not had to have our picnic sitting on
     the banks of the South Norton Y swimming pool
If only my engine too had shine-in-the-coal between
     the wild cherry trees
If only I had asked the girl on the train what she meant
     when she said 'If only the curl stays in my hair
     until midnight'
If only I could read without glasses I could have
     followed the handbook directions for distress
     signals
If only I had put more hearts on the Valentine dragon
     for Jill
If only I had never jumped over the city in the
     half day light

Complaint

Ah me!

I am the sea

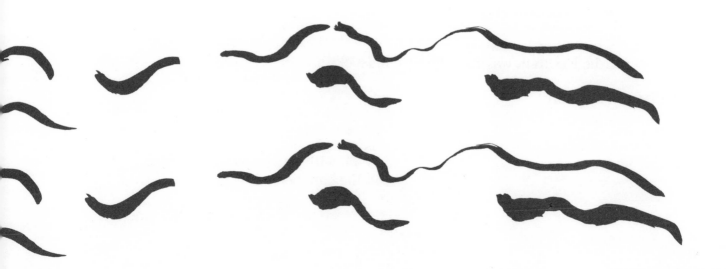

Ballet for Peaches

Donkey: What a Poet wants is Chicago covered
        with peaches

the Poet covered with peaches flies
        onto the stage

the Donkey climbs aboard and together
        they disappear into a wildrice moonset

        where shortly they are joined by
Images of Mr. Einstein waving hello with his socks

the Images multiply

A Show A Play: It's a girl!

a station
boy and girl
train enters
much kissing between boy and girl adieu goodby a little weeping
farewell
boy climbs on train
station exits with girl

a station
hundreds of people
train enters
all the people climb onto the train
station exits

o parted lovers
soliloquies o
suicide from cliffs that are leaping
o foxes pretending to be men

the ocean is a novel of wild lace and young dragons
a mountain is pink
air fresh
station empty
enter train
hundreds of passengers get off with picnic baskets and singing
train exits with landscape
the hundreds of passengers begin kissing each other
the station master the telegraph officer
the ticket seller the news stand woman the
oranges the boards of the platform the
barnswallow nests in the rafters over the
benches the timetables the trash disposal boxes
the mail slit the cigarette machine the telephone
booth the telephone the numbers on the dial the
holes for putting your finger in the ceiling the
cobwebs the new green paint the sign saying
women the sign saying men the boxes of red geraniums
planted by the Women of Darien the radiators the
heat the dust the cigarette butts the ashes
the ashes

a station
is empty
enter train
hundreds of trees get off

the ocean the ocean is a novel
a sword fight breaks out
Yoshitsune of The Thousand Cherry Blossom Trees
once again once again they die
once again they swords in hand
turn backward in their somersaults
the mountain is pink
fresh is the air
a station is empty
enter train of wild lace and young dragons get off
with picnic baskets of singing the station goes
away goodby farewell adieu and kisses
a little weeping are your wings
o boy o girl
o barnswallow nests in the rafters
                in the rafters

in the rafters a station
boy and girl
enter train weeping
adieu oranges they kiss goodby farewell
poor train once again
the station goes away
o station that went away the show goes on
o novel of wild dragons turning back somersaults in lace
o hundreds of fresh pink mountains
fresh is the air o
fresh is the air
fresh is o

Song of the Melancholy Dress

I stand among The Thousand Cherry Blossom People
the air is swords and broken
where is the ocean the wild
where is the lace the dragons where
and the station that went away
where is the mountain where
is the train is it vanquished again and turning
backward o backward in
back somersaults
where are the red geraniums planted by the Women of Darien where
o my station that went away my ocean o
my novel my pink mountain my young dragons

o parted lovers soliloquies o
suicide from cliffs that are leaping
o foxes pretending to be men

Dante and the Poet

POET: in a poem
you make your point with—

DANTE flies onto the stage
from all directions
the urinating multitudes electrocute themselves
and the landscape becomes

DARK CLOSETS full of no light fly on take over

NARRATOR
night falls is it a shell yes
the shell opens
seven ladies in bright kimonos
are seated as if pearls

CHORUS OF LADIES
this is your house, Onward,
will you come in
costume motion verse and music
every part of you we invite
like a favorite avacado vine

NARRATOR
and gradually they are telling her they tell her
a story
to seduce her

LEADER OF THE CHORUS OF LADIES
once-upon-a-time—

ALL THE LADIES TOGETHER
once-upon-a-time—

Onward

NARRATOR
Onward, the protagonist, steps into the shell
listening to the roar
she is laughing to keep time
her body is moving as if about to dance
the north of her is green

the seven ladies in bright kimonos
are still seated as if pearls
the shell closes
night goes up in flame is it the sleeves
of the kimono of the sun yes

News

Miss Diana Palmer went roaring through a ceremony tonight of white lace whips waving wild and hurtling with winds of eighty miles an hour or more over the top of the Wedding March straight to the bottom of Christ Church (Baptist) with Mr. Theodore Van Huston. This was her maiden voyage.

Song

When your boyfriend writes you a letter
and you light up the air it's
love

When your boyfriend writes and you run
and the road runs with you and you run to the sea
the big blue beautiful bounding sea
and you tear it up the letter the beautiful letter
so your mother can't read it or find it no never
you jump with it into the sea
                                        the sea
you jump with it into the mighty fine sea

When your boyfriend writes
When your boyfriend writes
and you light up the air
you light up the road
your shoes light up
your hair lights up it's
love oh-h-h-h-h-h-h it' –
s-s-s-s-s LOVE

Molly
Apollinaire trying to translate himself into English
New York Poetry Student
Catalogue of Philosophy Courses

Quartet

MOLLY
yes

APOLLINAIRE
the garden of the song
bats itself like flowers

MOLLY
I said yes

APOLLINAIRE
in the wind
who bats like flowers

MOLLY
I will Yes

APOLLINAIRE
batting in the wind

PHILOSOPHY CATALOGUE
the pre-Socratic School .
and the Vedas

MOLLY
and the sea the sea
crimson sometimes like fire

POETRY STUDENT
Farina of my heart with atomic lyric of lump
You electrify me more than a sixteen-story sonnetful
       of astro-camera-cognac

APOLLINAIRE
the garden of the troops
sings very sweetly
while slowly the cows
are abandoned

POETRY STUDENT
You are the missile-piece in my son-of-a-cream-of-stanza

MOLLY
and the fig tree in the Alameda gardens yes
and all the queer little streets
and pink and blue and yellow houses

PHILOSOPHY CATALOGUE
Plato and the Upanishads

MOLLY
and Gibraltar as a girl where I was a flower of the mountain

APOLLINAIRE
like a masque of tyranny
memories sound
among the winds
I shall return to myself often

PHILOSOPHY CATALOGUE
the Indianism of Jesus
the Buddhism of the Essenes

POETRY STUDENT
the happy-go-boiled-again of my consonance

MOLLY
like the Andalusian girls

APOLLINAIRE
and so much of the universe is forgotten
where is Christopher Columbus
who owes us the unmemorizing of continence
and takes so seriously phantoms

MOLLY
going about serene with his lamp
yes and then we'd have a hospital nurse next thing
on the carpet and O

POETRY STUDENT
My cracked bean of galaxy-enjambement
My purée of pentameter in a pink parachute

PHILOSOPHY CATALOGUE
Islam and the West
Thoreau and his contemporaries

APOLLINAIRE
the Don Juan of a thousand and three comets ha!

MOLLY
and how he kissed me under the Moorish wall

POETRY STUDENT
You a anapest are in constellation of mush

APOLLINAIRE
toujours

PHILOSOPHY CATALOGUE
the Hinduism of Turgenev
Tolstoy
Dostoyevsky
Gorky
England-Ireland
the impact of the East on Yeats
T. S. Eliot
Aldous Huxley

APOLLINAIRE
toujours

MOLLY
I thought as well him as another

POETRY STUDENT
A salad-ballad in bullet and
capsule of hexameter-corn

PHILOSOPHY CATALOGUE
Egyptian philosophy
Indian thought

APPOLLINAIRE
let us pass
all passes

MOLLY
all perfume yes
and his heart was going like mad

APPOLLINAIRE
toujours toujours
it makes a little heavy
and your hair
so long, Marie
which gives an air
of going to adventure

News

A young man in scanty contemplation clad was picked up yester-night while undergoing a dialect change at the junction of Second Avenue and St. Germaine. He is said to be the first of the season.

Re-examination of Freedom

ONE
If I were FREEDOM
I'd enter the mountains
and run like a waterfall

Two
If I were FREEDOM
I'd be that mud puddle
where Walter Raleigh laid his cloak
no I mean I'd be that cloak
laid by Sir Walter in the puddle of Queen Elizabeth I mean
the puddle for Queen Elizabeth I mean
once there was a puddle and there was a queen and
along came Sir Walter Somethingorother and laid down his cloak
for her
if I were FREEDOM
I'd be that cloak
and the World my Queen
I mean

THREE
If I were FREEDOM
I'd take off I'd fly
most beautiful I
would range in the sky
another sun
and the people sunflowers

ALL
If I
If I
and
If I

SONG

If I were FREEDOM
I'd love you
in the demented batteries
I'd love you
on the sidewalk
I'd love you
and glasses are empty but
I'd love you I'd love you

abandoned thus to the fury of symbols
If I were FREEDOM
and suddenly there is the wilderness
I'd love you
yes all hands are lost when the ship goes down but
I'd love you
the shadows crowd on the shore
I love you
tell me before the ferryman's return
I love you I love you
and everything is full of the sea

If I were FREEDOM
I'd love you
dirty calabash
I'd love you
my lion
I'd love you I'd love you
if I were FREEDOM
on feathers in my head if there were snow
on cards on the tables on the chairs
the waves distill you
and the night

salt white stuff on stones
I love you
so that one discovers strawberries at the rim of fire everyday
I love you I love you
which is a condition that becomes a festival

Questions or maybe Answers

CHILD
Mother, in autumn do bricks
fall the way leaves do?

MOTHER
No, dear.

(child goes off—theatre falls)

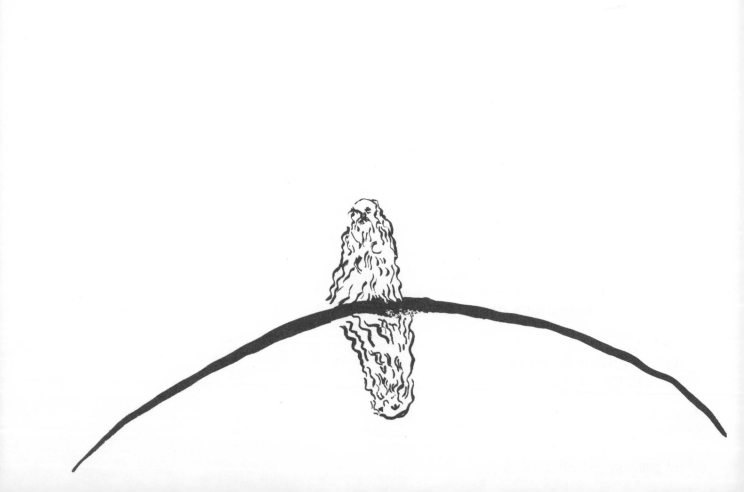

There's a little ambiguity over there
among the bluebells

ONE: What a poet wants is a lake in the middle
of his sentence
(a lake appears)

TWO: yes and a valid pumpkin
(a pumpkin appears)

THREE: and you should slice up language like a
meatcutter abba dabba dabba dabba yack
(sliced up language appears)

FOUR: It's fine we have inhibitions
otherwise we'd all be dead
(all drop dead)

FIVE: or flat on our backs
(all roll over onto backs)

SIX: yes and everyone on rollerskates in bed
would be nice
(everyone on rollerskates in bed appears)

SEVEN: and a delayed verb

EIGHT: and an old upright piano
(an old upright piano appears)

(all bow together to the audience and to each other)

NINE: goes to the piano and begins to play
(everyone dances)

There's a little ambiguity

ONE: What a poet wants is a lake in the middle
of his sentence
(a lake appears)

an avalanche appears
an earthquake appears
a hurricane appears
my feelings are a lake
the strategy of lakes is infinite

— Ruth Krauss

Several people were asked how they would stage
Speech One from the title poem...

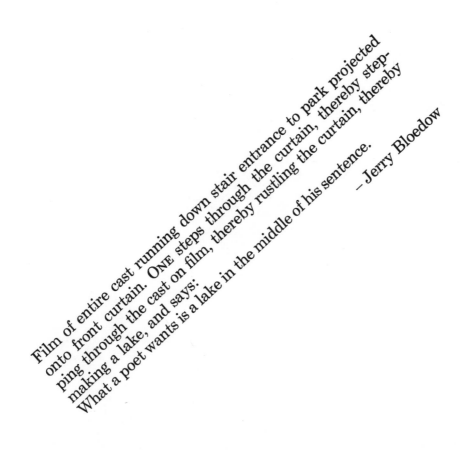

Film of entire cast running down stair entrance to park projected onto front curtain. ONE steps through the curtain, thereby stepping through the cast on film, thereby rustling the curtain, thereby making a lake, and says:
What a poet wants is a lake in the middle of his sentence.

— Jerry Bloedow

[Speaker is perhaps dressed in a business-suit, grey-flannel, black shined shoes, black socks, white shirt, conservative tie, has relatively long hair with daisies in it.] [or feminine equivalent, black dress, string of pearls]

" . . . of his sentence"

Slide is projected on screen center stage, large as possible but clear, of a lake (Lake Tahoe, for example), but sideways, so that water is to the right, mountains, trees to the left. A stage-worker, behind screen, not to side (dressed in black if slide does not show on him, in white if it does), pours from a bucket (white if bucket intercepts projected picture, black if it doesn't) water through *lake part of projection*, into a *metal* (or *wooden*, may be better, but *not plastic*) wash-tub on floor. When last drip ends (5 seconds at most, don't wait for very last drip) blackout (except on speaker, or as arranged by director). Whole thing quick & snappy.

– George Brecht

WHAT A POET WANTS IS A

IN THE MIDDLE OF HIS SENTENCE

Remy Charlip

Spotlight on a Stove.

Voice (offstage): What a poet wants is a lake in the middle of his sentence.

Cook enters. Second spot falls on People at a Table, forks in fists, prongs up. Cook removes a huge Cake from the oven. It's a map of the USA. Ignoring the body of the cake, she carefully cuts off the frosting from the top, and gives some to each person at the table—but only the Great Lakes. The rest is thrown away. Ornamental Mirror may be tilted to show this to Audience.

— Dick Higgins

Blackout.

for television

A field in Vietnam. Shots & mortar fire. Men running & crouching.
A medic crouches over a young soldier lying in the grass. The medic
is breathing into the young soldier's mouth – repeatedly – he tries
to revive the wounded man. Finally he gives up. The man is dead.

Walter Cronkite's voice is heard:

"What a poet wants is a lake in the
middle of his sentence."

Rain falls on the corpse of the young soldier.

– Peter Levin

Performed as part of a full piece called "The Cantilever Rainbow," at Café la Mama, in April 1965. Music by Don Heckman. Directed by Lawrence Sacharow.

The title of the poem-play "Ambiguity" is on a roller with other titles of plays by Ruth Krauss, which were done as one piece. In a music interlude, actor who is ONE turns the title roller in rhythm to the music, he is standing on a platform. Music stops, Actor ONE (Peter Berry) standing on a platform dressed in Derby Hat and cane, delivers line "What a poet wants is a lake in the middle of his sentence," assuming the role of the poet. Actors Two, THREE, and FOUR who are girls (Arlene Rothlein, Yolande Bavan and Carol Lipis), are in a semi-circle below the poet. They grasp arms, and lean backwards forming a circle singing "a lake appears," as they become the lake. Actor ONE jumps into the center of their circle as the girls say "splash." Water ballet music comes on as all four swim around the stage in a water ballet dance in blue light. Their movement continues, suggesting the idea of the loveliness of a lake in poetic imagery. As the music stops they end up in their positions for the next line, "yes and a valid pumpkin."

— Lawrence Sacharow

House is dark

VOICE   What a poet wants is a lake in the middle of his sentence

Stagelights on

A prisoner sits fishing in the lake in the middle of his cell

Stagelights off

            *   *   *

Cell   Cutout weighted curtain or transparent curtain with painted
bars across stagefront

Prisoner   In blue workpants & shirt with stenciled numbers
Or stereotyped striped hat pants and shirt with numbers

Sitting   On a cot almost parallel to stage right but angled toward
center upstage

Lake   Huge blue balloon semi-inflated

— Frances Starr

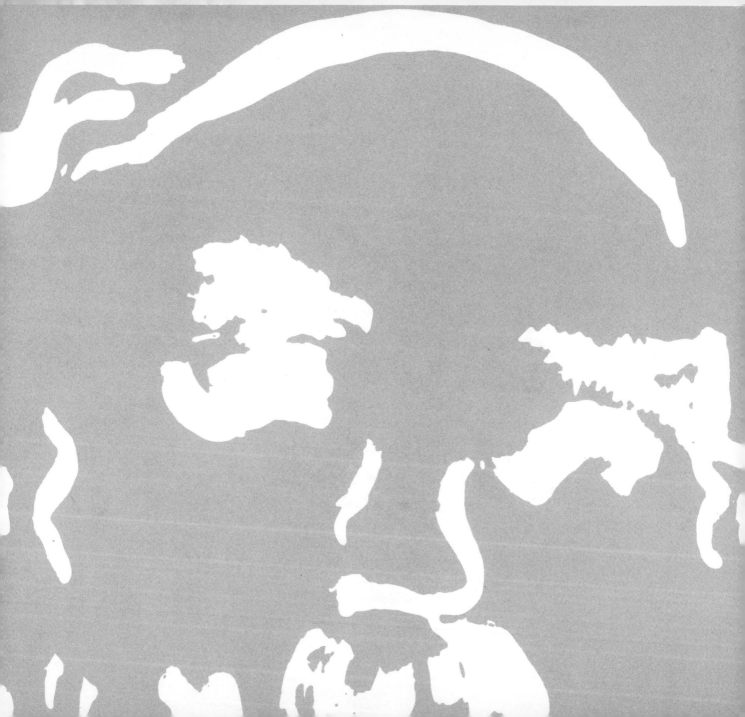

Questions or maybe Answers

in a cottage kitchen

CHILD: Mother, was a skyscraper
        once a little cottage
        like ours?

MOTHER: No, dear. Of course not.

(the COTTAGE begins to grow . . .

Uri Gagarin & William Shakespeare

compare thee
more lovely
and a single spin around the earth
winds do shake
withstanding well the state of weightlessness
too short
too hot
and often could see the earth my native
fair from fair sometime declines
through portholes no
by chance or
speed and changing course
shall not fade
I remember
possession of that fair
in my swift flight
covered in areas by clouds
and in his shade
eternal lines
alone
so long as men can breathe or eyes
so long
no falling continuously no

News

"This measure," the Attorney-General stated, "This legislation—which I endorse—requires some thirty thousand skylarks to register for the first time with my office." And he left the room.

If I were FREEDOM
I'd never be Aunt May
who thinks she is the U.S.A.
and her left leg is Florida

MAY: or is it my right
        no my left .
        I'll have a Civil War
        I'll sell Louisiana to Napoleon

LOUISIANA flies away

LEFT LEG: Napoleon Napoleon
            la la la la la——

Winnie-The-Pooh and William Shakespeare

Winnie: How sweet to be a cloud

W. S.: when daisies pied and violets

Winnie: floating in the blue

W. S.: and lady-smocks all silver-white
and cuckoo-buds of yellow hue

Winnie: Iniquum fatum fatu

W. S.: Cuckoo cuckoo cuckoo

Winnie: every little cloud
always sings aloud
it makes him very proud

W. S.: on every tree for thus sings he

Winnie: Winnie Ille Pu
Winnie Ille Pu

Together: Ecce Pu Ecce Pu
it makes him very proud
cuckoo cuckoo cuckoo
to paint the meadows with delight
to be a little cloud

SPRING running wild and throwing flowers
      comes upon the POET
      running wild and looking for a flower
      they collide

Practical Mother's Guide

BELL: begins ringing

CHILD: Mama Mama,
is that the bell for springtime?

MOTHER: No, silly, that's the door bell.
Would you answer it please.

DIRECTIONS: CHILD runs to the door

CHILD: Mama Mama, it's a man with the sun.

MOTHER: Well, dear, tell him to leave it.

CHILD: He says it's C.O.D.
And Mama, it's all tied up in ribbons and moths.

MOTHER: Ask him to bring it back tomorrow please.
We have no money in the house.

CHILD: Mama, he should leave it anyway.
It *was* the bell for springtime
and if we don't take it in but
send it away—
Mother Mother, the sun—
what will happen to it?

MOTHER: Well, I don't know.
            Shells are full of the sea
            the sea is full of waterbabies
            and if you look in the eyes of the waterbabies . . .
            . . . .
            Tell the man to take away the sun
            and bring you a waterbaby.

CHILD: Sir, we have no money for the C.O.D.
            Could you please leave the sun
            and it shine anyway?

MAN: Why not.
            Here.

DIRECTIONS: CHILD takes the sun
            and does a sun dance

The 50,000 Dogwood Trees at Valley Forge

HEADLINE: The 50,000 dogwood trees at Valley Forge are at the peak of their –

TREES: Bow! Wow! Wow!

HEADLINE: according to the Pennsylvania Department of Forests and Waters.
Special details of State Police have been assigned to –

POLICE: Bow! Wow! Wow!

HEADLINE: and to direct the –

AUTOMOBILES: Bow! Wow! Wow!

HEADLINE: automobiles –

TREES: Bow! Wow! Wow!
Bow! Wow! Wow!

POLICE: Bow! Wow! Wow!
Bow! Wow! Wow!

HEADLINE: Bow! Wow! Wow!
Bow! Wow! Wow!

ALL: Bow! Wow! Wow!
Wow! Wow! Wow!
Wow! Wow! Wow!
Wow! Wow! Wow!

A Beautiful Day

GIRL: What a beautiful day!

THE SUN falls down onto the stage

Duet

the day is so pretty

the umbrella is yellow

the day is so pretty
the sun is so shining

the umbrella is yellow
with white lace all around

the day is so yellow
the umbrella is so pretty
the sun is so all around
with white lace so shining

the umbrella is so yella
the sun is so pretty
with white all so shining
around lace so yellow umbrellow
with day is so yello sa yella
umbrella sa pretty sa yad

sa pretty sa yaddy
sa leylow sow lamu
brell white lace with shining
the sun is so all around

the day is so pretty
the umbrella is yellow
the day is so pretty
the sun is so shining
the umbrella is yellow
with white lace all around

ODE

A ballet by THINGS NAMED (rivers, buds, watermelons,
bird-shadows, bells, eyes, parades, groundhogs, pots,
ducks, mountains, strawberries, glaciers, wings, etcetera,
or as many as possible) is interwoven with the poem
spoken by the NAME-CALLER

"hot-maker   snow-melter   river-sweller

bud-buster   watermelon-ripener   pattern-maker-through-forest-trees-one

rooster-waker   people-browner   shadow-of-migrating-bird-maker

in-the-east-one   in-the-west-one   straight-up-one

neck-breaker   Moslem-bender   noodle-dryer

hypnotizer-of-morning-glories   bell-ringer   spitfire

made-small-shining-in-my-eye-one   parade-encourager   picnic-monger

democratic-one   undemocratic-one   silhouetter-of-tall-pines-in-the-air

candle-lighter   dragon-lighter   red-sky-at-evening-lighter

thunder-maker   groundhog-fooler   pot-boiler

who-threw-the-first-stone-one   Old-Sol   New-Sol

duck-sitting-on-own-self-in-lake-maker   Soleil   Eye-of-Mexico uns snu nussy shine-in-the-coal moon-hider

sky-cleaner and-makest-thou-the-wind-to-blow makest-thou-the-balloon-to-bust

the-streams-that-are-hot-in-the-cold-sea-maker leaf-turner century-turner

sky-ticker what-would-happen-if-you-skipped-a-day-one

blood-light vein-light bone-light

phoenix-imitator daisy-symbol Indian-giver

apple-on-the-head-of-Sir-Isaac-hitter on-the-topmost-tip-of-the-mast-gleam

old-dogtail-wagger shady-side-of-the-street-maker shine-on-shoe-maker

in-the puddles-one in-the-tide lighting-the-mountain

right-at-my-own-doorstep-you-are-one stoop-sitter moth-maker

lunchtime-bringer bogeyman-assistant old-x-behind-the-x-ray

to-stud-nightfall-with-sparks-one old-sunnyside-up-in-the sky pretty-day

bringer-of-bluebells buttercup-yellower strawberry-reddener

dark-horse-of-another-color who-saw-the-Golden-Age-one

second-fiddle-to-Nero glacier-giver engine-driver

devil-driver wingtip-lighter old-hotstuff"

Derangement

Human derangement is order in the universe and
who am I to upset it

NARRATOR: in a poem you make your point with pineapples

PINEAPPLES fly onto the stage from all directions

SPY: and it would be nice to have a spy going in and out

This Breast

This breast Mexican poetry
This breast Chinese history
This breast Odyssey

This breast Eugénie Grandet at the age of seven
This breast a resort in the Black Forest
This breast was acquainted with the King of Monataccata
This breast given special permission to settle in Geneva
This breast Dostoevskian Masterpiece

This breast Hegelian
This breast little acorn does to mighty oak tree grow

This breast as the Irish Statesman so shrewdly remarked
                most unabashed explorer of the crypts of the soul
This breast—but we have nothing but the word of Mr. Snooks
This breast a dove
This breast the flower of Gum Swamp
This breast a little confused by this possibility
This breast suggesting by turns the mother the mistress
                the father the Church Ireland India Greenland
                Tierra del Fuego and the boot of Italy
This breast apostrophe to the cathedral of night

This breast Olé

This breast Shakespeare
This breast Picasso
This breast Einstein
This breast I seen it in the papers

This breast in Egypt the Pharoah
This breast we must emphasize the fact that a man should bid
        farewell before going to his death
This breast with the historic city near the entrance to
        the Hellespont
This breast composed entirely of scraps of historic fact
This breast giant devil troll sorcerer cannibal
This breast earliest form of the ballad in France
This breast the field and wood blossom thereat

This breast would you like to know how it started
This breast then we shall have to take an exciting trip
This breast boom-boom yippee slurp strawberries cabañas
This breast as we go whizzing along
This breast thousands of years go by
This breast we have a fine view of everything that happens
This breast like the time the star
This breast there has also been some attempt to correlate
        its activity with changes in the time of the
        migration of swallows with wheat yields and
        even with social revolutions
This breast suddenly
        waves quiverings storms lightnings shining
        music apple-blossoms green grass blue days
        little forget-me-nots

This breast surveyors at first considered flatlands
This breast the train service was never there
This breast following the dedication service there will be
                a reception for old-timers
This breast serve as a reminder of the famous Railroad
                That Went Totemic
This breast celebration parades fiesta a circus state-of-
                the-state message one touch-down favorite
                walloped the Philadephia Eagles U.S. representatives
                on the scene should have ah-ha! Doe not mock me
                in thy bed while these cold nights freeze me dead
                in the supernatural dark of Main Street West
                under the trestle with dreams broke down
                tobacco haze

This breast volta! he is suddenly galvanized by the announcement
This breast to go to a special performance
This breast of predilection
                the legendary radiance the wanton
This breast between the final stations of revolutionary orbit
                no day no night summer or winter thermal radiation
                transmissions megacycles and as to the Eastern
                flank the encroachment of the North American
                continent complicates matters
This breast needs timetable
This breast early one morning Gothic, Gothic on a vernal sea

News

"Cuckoo cuckoo cuckoo," president of the Young Cuckoo's Christian Association board said today during the appointment of a married man as general chairman of the YCCA's local $800,000 building and expansion campaign. "When daisies pied and violets blue," the president continued, "Cuckoo cuckoo cuckoo cuckoo." The president's speech will be repeated again tonight in a nation-wide broadcast.

Miracle or Goodbye My Poets' Storefront

POET
What a poet wants is
the ID in the middle of a sentence

NARRATOR
the ID appears and
begins to roar it is roaring like a dogstar under the moon
it is rising is the sea yes the air yes the constellation
of the –

CHORUS OF SAILING SHIPS, LIONS, LADDERS THAT LEAP, MR. EINSTEIN,
AND CHILDREN OF THE LEPER-COLONY KINDERGARTEN AT THAT
MOMENT WHEN THEY ARE RUNNING DOWN THE SIDES OF THE
ERUPTING VOLCANO WHO IS SINKING FOREVER LIKE GRANDMOTHER
THE ONE THE FIRE-DEPARTMENT HAD TO BE CALLED IN TO
PICK UP WHEN SHE FELL
yes yes yes yes yes yes

NARRATOR
yes roaring rising fills the stage that is
the auditorium the poet – he bows –

POET
Gangway!

NARRATOR
and rises a balloon the poet flying away whoops
the audience a thousand balloons the theatre rising whoops whoops
flying away goodbye my love my own farewell
and kisses
Cornelia Street

in a Bull's Eye

1500 HORSES rush by going east in profile

1500 HORSES rush by going west in profile

1500 HORSES rush by going east again in profile

GIRL begins undressing

FIRE breaks out

CROWD rolls over a cliff

MAN: It's very hot I'll leave my hat and jacket here*

BATTLESHIP sinks

BULL'S EYE closes

*line from *An American Tragedy*

IMITATION

in the womb the wombmen come and go

POET: in a poem
　　　you make your point with –

AN OCEAN rises with a boat and a sail

the POET goes sailing away

water song?

POET: in a poem
       you make your point with a flower

A SLICE OF PIE appears

POET eats PIE

YUM-YUM BOY: yum yum

POET: in a poem
            you make your point with a flower

A BOTTLE OF WINE flies over

BOTTLE: from France

POET: Ah! from France

POET opens BOTTLE and drinks

shortly FLOWERS-IN-THE-HEAD

together they the POET et LES FLEURS DE FRANCE
do a drunk-flower dance

FRENCH POET: in a poem
              one makes one's point with
              skies of quicksilver and nubile under the water
              buttocks of sandstone –

FRENCH COOK: in a poem
              one makes one's point with
              egg mixture as in basic omelette
              one tablespoon fresh chopped chives
              one tablespoon fresh chopped basil
              one tablespoon fresh chopped tarragon PRESTO!
              and a bottle of dry white wine

the COOK places the omelette around the POET who
sits there amiably after properly embracing the COOK and
TOGETHER they eat the cook-poem

COOK: ah!

POET: ah! ah!

Song

        basil and tarragon
        buttocks and wine
        skies of quicksilver
        lalalala –

FLOWER: in a poem
          you make your point with a poet

MANY POETS fly onto the stage like firecrackers
          from everywhere they –

FLOWER: Help!

FLOWER rises in a small flame
          and falls in ashes as

the POETS crash together in a heap on that spot

AN ASHCAN appears

and the moon
is set upon by Tarzan with his fan

POET: in a poem
     you make your point with a flower

AN ASHCAN appears

          CURTAINS

POET: in a poem
you make your point with a flower

AN ASHCAN appears

ASHCAN: The poet is thinking

POET: in a poem
you make your point with an ashcan

MANY ASHCANS fly onto the stage from all directions they
knock the POET out

POET: in a poem
        you make your point with a flower

AN ASHCAN appears

POET droops

SECOND ASHCAN appears

POET droops more

DOZENS OF ASHCANS appears

POET cannot droops further farther

FIRST ASHCAN begins to dance

SECOND ASHCAN begins to dance

MUSIC?

ALL THE ASHCANS begins to dance they do the ashcan-can

POET begins to dance

POET: in a poem
        you make your point with a flower

AN ASHCAN appears

POET takes paintbrush and paints flowers over ASHCAN

CURTAINS pour down disguised as rain

POET: in a poem
         you make your point with a flower

NOTHING happens

we wait he waits the POET

IT begins to rain

POET gets wet

BIG SUN comes out

in Granada

A FLOWER

mounted on mother-of-pearl

A FLOWER

without bridle or stirrups

POET: in a poem
you make your point with a flower

FLOWERS fly in from all directions and are

CURTAINS

FLOWER: in a poem
           you make your point with a poet

A POET appears

SUCCESS comes leaping like Tarzan
          and bows

FLOWER and POET embrace

POET: in a poem
 you make your point with –

the FLOOR rises under the POET and
 crashes through to the night outside

STARS: in a poem
 you make your point with –

the POET bows and shines from up there among the STARS

CHORUS OF ASTRONOMERS: Eureka!

Weather

Drizzle tonight off the east coast of my head.